HOW DID WE
FIND OUT ABOUT
THE SPEED OF LIGHT ?

The "HOW DID WE FIND OUT . . . ?" SERIES
by Isaac Asimov

HOW DID WE
FIND OUT ABOUT
THE SPEED OF LIGHT?

Isaac Asimov
Illustrated by David Wool

Walker and Company
New York

First published in the United States of America
in 1986 by the Walker Publishing Company, Inc.

Published simultaneously in Canada by John Wiley & Sons
Canada, Limited, Rexdale, Ontario.

Library of Congress Cataloging-in-Publication Data

Asimov, Isaac, 1920-
　How did we find out about the speed of light?

(The "How did we find out—?" series)
Includes index.
　Summary: Traces the scientific study of the speed of
light, from Galileo's experiments in the seventeenth
century to more recent discoveries involving the law
of relativity.
　1. Light—Speed—Juvenile literature. [1. Light—
Speed] I. Wool, David, ill. II. Title. III. Series:
Asimov, Isaac, 1920-　. How did we find out—series.
QC407.A85　1986　　535'.24　　86-4085
ISBN 0-8027-6637-4
ISBN 0-8027-6613-7 (lib. bdg.)

Printed in the United States of America

10 9 8 7 6 5 4 3 2

Contents

To Joshua Guarino
who, I'm sure,
will be reading my books someday.

1
The First
Determination

HAVE YOU EVER seen a lightning flash during a thunderstorm?

Lightning is a current of electricity that races from the ground to a cloud, or from one cloud to another. As it does so, it heats to a white-hot temperature of many thousands of degrees for a split-second, and the air expands. When the lightning flash is over, the air cools and contracts again, coming together with a bang. That bang is the clap of thunder we hear.

When the lightning strikes fairly close to us, the flash of lightning is very bright and the clap of thunder is very loud, and they come at the same time.

When the lightning is far away, it flashes not so brightly and it does so silently. If we wait a while, however, the thunder comes, echoing and re-echoing, but it is not so loud.

It is reasonable to suppose that a distant lightning flash is not as bright as a near one and that the thunder is not as loud — but why is there a wait for the thunder?

It is because it takes time for sound to travel from one place to another. The speed of sound has been measured and found to be 740 miles per hour.

This means that sound can travel 1,086 feet in one second. In five seconds, sound can travel a mile. If a lightning flash strikes a mile away, you have to wait five seconds for the sound of the thunder to reach you. If it strikes two miles away, you have to wait ten seconds for it to reach you, and so on.

But what about the light of the lightning flash? Doesn't *that* take time to reach you, too?

Perhaps it does, but if so, it must travel much faster than sound, because the sight of the lightning reaches us quite a bit of time before the thunder does.

Is there any way we can measure how fast light travels?

In ancient times there was a general feeling that one couldn't. Some scholars thought light might travel so fast that it would cover any distance, however long, in just an instant of time. It might travel at "infinite" speed; that is, faster than any speed you can imagine.

Even those scholars who thought the speed of light was *not* infinite, still thought it was too fast for it to be measured.

The first person who tried to measure the speed of light was an Italian scientist, Galileo (gahl-ih-LAY-oh, 1564-1642). He made the attempt about 1630.

He and an assistant each carried lanterns of a kind

Galileo's experiment with the speed of light

in which the candle inside could be covered and un-
covered, so that the light could be flashed at a particular time. On a dark night, when small gleams of
light could be easily seen, Galileo and his assistant
climbed two neighboring hills. When each got to the
top of his hill, each flashed his light so the other could
see he was there. Once each saw the other's lantern,
both lanterns were closed.

Now Galileo flashed his lantern. The instant his
assistant on the other hill saw Galileo's light, he
flashed *his* lantern. Galileo measured the time between the moment he flashed his lantern and the
moment he saw his assistant's flash (perhaps by

counting off seconds). The test was repeated a number of times probably and the results were averaged. The amount of time that passed had to be at least partly due to the time it took light to travel from one hilltop to the other, and then back.

It was also partly due to "reaction time." After all, it took some time after the assistant saw Galileo's flash to realize that he had seen it, and to move his hand in such a way as to uncover his own flash.

Galileo then repeated the experiment by making use of two hills that were considerably farther apart than the first pair. Galileo felt that his assistant's reaction time would be the same as before, but now the light would have to travel a longer distance. The extra time it would take between Galileo's flash and his sight of the return flash would be entirely due to the time taken for the light to travel the extra distance.

However, there was *no extra time.* The time taken between flashes when the two hills were distant was exactly the same as when the two hills were close. It was all reaction time. The light itself travelled so swiftly that the extra time taken to travel the longer distance was too small for Galileo to measure. All Galileo could say was that light traveled very, very fast.

—(Of course, Galileo was at a disadvantage for he had no way of measuring short periods of time accurately. Good clocks had not yet been invented.)

In 1609, Galileo, making use of the first telescope ever to be turned on the sky, had discovered four satellites of Jupiter. These satellites revolved around

Jupiter. Each one would move in front of Jupiter, then move outward in one direction, return and move behind Jupiter, then move outward in the other direction, then return again and move in front of Jupiter and so on, over and over.

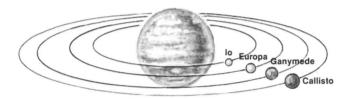

Jupiter and four of its moons

Each time one of the satellites went behind Jupiter, it moved into "eclipse," and since they each moved about Jupiter at a steady speed, they went into eclipse at fixed intervals. The satellite nearest Jupiter swung about in the shortest time, going into eclipse every $1\frac{3}{4}$ days. The next farther went into eclipse every $3\frac{1}{2}$ days, the next every $7\frac{1}{6}$ days, and the farthest every $16\frac{3}{4}$ days.

In 1656, a Dutch astronomer, Christiaan Huygens (HOI-genz, 1629-1695) invented the pendulum clock, making use of certain properties of the pendulum that Galileo had discovered. It was the first accurate timepiece ever built, the first that could measure time to the exact minute. It could be used to time events such as the eclipses of Jupiter's satellites more accurately than before.

A Dutch astronomer, Olaus Roemer (ROI-mer, 1644-1710), studied Jupiter's satellites in this way, and made a puzzling discovery. He noticed that during half of the year, the eclipses came later and later than their scheduled time, and then started coming earlier and earlier. In the course of the whole year, the eclipses came at the right time *on the average*, but there were times when they were as much as 8 minutes ahead of the average and other times when they were as much as 8 minutes behind the average.

Why should that be?

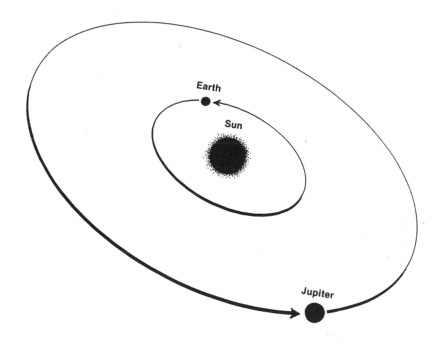

Orbits of Earth and Jupiter

The Earth goes around the Sun, making a circle in one year. Jupiter is much farther from the Sun and makes a larger circle. It takes 12 years to complete that circle.

The Earth goes around the Sun twelve times while Jupiter is going around once. That means that during half its year, Earth is on the same side of the Sun as Jupiter, and, during the other half, it is on the opposite side.

When the Earth is on the same side of the Sun as Jupiter, and is as close as it can be to the other planet, light travels from Jupiter's satellites to Earth across a certain distance. Half a year later, Earth is on the other side of its orbit, and is therefore on the opposite side of the Sun from Jupiter. The light from Jupiter's satellites must then travel the same distance as before, *plus* an extra distance across the width of Earth's orbit.

It takes time for light to cross the full width of the Earth's orbit. Astronomers on Earth must wait that extra time before they see the eclipse of Jupiter's satellite. That is why the eclipse is later than average then. When Earth is on the same side as Jupiter, the light travels a comparatively short distance and the eclipses are earlier than average.

The exact width of Earth's orbit was not yet known in Roemer's time. Roemer took the best figure he knew for that width and decided that light must take about 16 minutes to cross that distance. To travel that distance in that time, Roemer calculated that light must move at a speed of 132,000 miles per second.

Because Roemer had the wrong figure for the width of Earth's orbit, he ended up with a speed of light that was considerably lower than it should have been. In fact, it was over 50,000 miles per second too low—but it was a remarkable result for a first effort.

Still, even Roemer's figure, which he announced in 1676, was extremely fast. No wonder Galileo couldn't measure the speed of light by timing it from one hill to another. If the hills were a mile apart, light would travel from one to the other and back (assuming Roemer's figure was correct) in $\frac{1}{60,000}$ of a second. If the hills were ten miles apart, light would flash from one to the other and back in $\frac{1}{6000}$ of a second. Galileo couldn't possibly have measured such small fractions of a second.

2
From Space to Earth

ROEMER'S ANNOUNCEMENT DIDN'T make much of a splash. The speed seemed so huge that people couldn't imagine it. Or perhaps the idea of using a clock to measure time so accurately still seemed strange to people. In any case, Roemer's work was largely forgotten and nothing happened to call it back to mind for about 70 years.

Meanwhile, scientists had become interested in another subject. The stars were known to be very far away, but no one knew exactly how far they might be. As the Earth went around the Sun, however, it shifted its position enormously.

From one side of the Sun a nearby star might be seen in the sky at a certain separation from a far-off star. From the other side of the Sun (six months later), that nearby star would be viewed from a slightly different angle and it would seem a slightly different separation from that same far-off star. (The far-off star would be so far away that the whole shift in Earth's position would be as nothing in comparison. The far-off star would, therefore, not change position at all.)

This shift in position of a nearby star compared to a far-off one as the Earth's position in space changes is called "parallax" (PAR-uh-laks). You can see how it works if you place your finger about a foot in front of your face and hold it steady there. If you close your left eye, you will see the finger with your right eye near a certain object in the background (a tree outdoors, a lamp indoors). Now without moving your finger, open your left eye and close your right. Viewing the finger with your left eye, which is in a different position from your right, you will see it in a different position with respect to the tree or the lamp.

From the amount of the shift, it is possible to calculate the distance of the finger from your eyes. In the same way, from the amount of the shift of the nearby star as the Earth swings about the Sun, astronomers can calculate the distance of the star.

The trouble was, though, that even the nearest stars are so far off that their parallaxes are tiny. The telescopes of the 1700s were simply not good enough to be able to measure those tiny parallaxes. However, scientists didn't know this and they kept on trying to measure the position of stars in the course of the year and to note any changes.

One of those who did so was the English astronomer, James Bradley (1693-1762). Through his

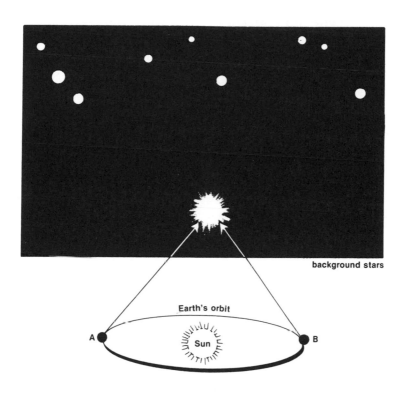

background stars

Earth's orbit

A   Sun   B

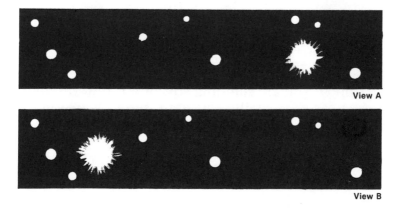

View A

View B

Parallax

telescope he did notice a small shift in the position of certain stars as the Earth swung around the Sun.

The shifts weren't right though. As the Earth moved in one direction, the position of the star should seem to shift in the opposite direction. The shift that Bradley observed didn't do that. The star shifted in the wrong direction, so it couldn't be parallax.

But if it wasn't parallax, what was it?

Bradley puzzled over the matter and eventually he came up with this idea.

Suppose you are standing still in a rainstorm, and the raindrops are falling straight down. If you have an umbrella, you would hold it directly over your head and that would keep you dry.

But suppose you begin to walk forward in such a rainstorm. A raindrop that would just miss your umbrella would hit you for as it moves lower you would walk into it. Therefore, once you move, you would have to angle your umbrella forward just a little so that raindrops will miss you farther in front than in back. After all, you are walking toward the raindrops in front, and away from the raindrops in back.

The faster you move, the further forward you will have to angle the umbrella, for if you move faster, you must make the raindrops miss you by a greater amount so that your faster motion won't carry you into them.

Again, if the raindrops are falling more slowly, you will have to angle your umbrella further forward because there is more time for you to walk into a raindrop falling slowly, than one falling rapidly.

You can calculate the exact amount you must angle your umbrella if you know both your own speed and the speed of the raindrops and compare the two. In reverse, if you know the exact angle that the umbrella requires to keep you dry, and you know how fast you are moving, then you can calculate how fast the raindrops must be falling.

It occurred to Bradley that light from a star must fall down upon the Earth like raindrops. However, the Earth is not standing still but is moving around the Sun. Because it is, the telescope has to be angled just a bit to catch the light, just as an umbrella must be angled to catch the raindrops. As the Earth curves in its turn about the Sun, the star would shift just in the way that Bradley had seen them shift.

Bradley knew exactly by how much the telescope had to be angled to catch the starlight, because that amounted to the shift of the star and he could measure that. He also knew how fast the Earth was moving about the Sun. From these two figures he could calculate the speed with which the light was moving as it fell from the star to the Earth.

His figure, which he reported in 1748, turned out to be 176,000 miles per second. This was considerably better than Roemer's figure, but it was still about 10,000 miles per second too low.

Astronomers were a great deal readier to deal with such an enormous figure in Bradley's time than in Roemer's. For the first time, the speed of light was accepted as having a particular value.

Both Roemer's and Bradley's method for calculating the speed of light involved astronomical events— the time it took light to go from Jupiter to Earth, or the direction in which light fell from a star to Earth.

Was there a way of moving the technique from space to Earth? Could scientists measure the speed of light on Earth, so that adjustments could be made easily and so that all sorts of details could be determined?

In 1849, this was done, when a French scientist, Armand Hippolyte Fizeau (fee-ZOH, 1819-1896) decided to repeat Galileo's experiment—with improvements.

As Galileo had done, Fizeau chose two hilltops, and in his case they were five miles apart. Fizeau managed to avoid the problem of reaction time, however. Instead of putting an assistant on the second hill, he put a mirror there.

A beam of light would be released by Fizeau on the first hill. It would flash to the second hill and be reflected by the mirror *at once* and flash back to Fizeau again. From the time between the moment the flash was sent out and the moment it came back, one would know the exact time it would take light to travel ten miles, and from that one could easily calculate the speed of light.

But enough was known about the speed of light by now to know that the time-lapse would be about $\frac{1}{18,000}$ of a second. Fizeau had better timepieces than Galileo had had, but still he couldn't measure a time-lapse *that* tiny, unless he used some clever method.

Fizeau used a very clever method indeed.

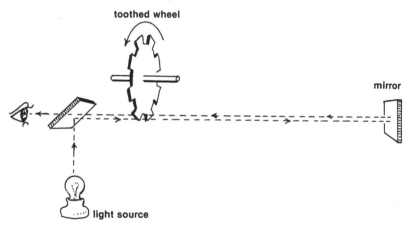

Fizeau's attempt to measure the speed of light

He made use of a toothed wheel, the edge of which he placed in front of his light beam. Whether the light beam got through the edge of the wheel depended on the wheel's position. If one of the teeth was directly in front of the light beam, it was blocked. If a gap between the teeth was in front of the light beam, it got through.

Fizeau set the toothed wheel spinning at a slow speed. If a flash of light shot through one of the gaps, it travelled to the mirror on the hilltop five miles away, was reflected from the mirror, then travelled back to Fizeau so quickly that the gap was still in place. The wheel had not had time to move the gap and place a tooth in the way of the beam of light to block it.

Fizeau made the toothed wheel move faster and faster. When the wheel turned at a certain speed, the light would move from Fizeau through a gap to the other hill where it would be reflected. By the time the beam had moved back to Fizeau, however, the tooth had moved across and blocked the light from returning to Fizeau's eye.

If Fizeau continued to make the wheel spin faster and faster, then, eventually, the light would shoot through a gap and, by the time it travelled five miles to the other hill and five miles back, the tooth had moved completely across the line of sight. The beam of light returned in time to move through the *next* gap and Fizeau could see it again.

Fizeau knew how fast the wheel was turning, so he knew how much time it took for a tooth to replace a gap, and how much time for a tooth to move completely across so that a second gap replaced the first one. He could calculate the time it took light to move ten miles and from that he could calculate the speed of light.

Fizeau's 1849 calculation placed the speed of light at 196,000 miles per second. For the first time, someone had found a value that was too high. Actually,

Fizeau's value was no better than Bradley's. Bradley's value had been 10,000 miles per second too slow, and Fizeau's was 10,000 miles per second too high.

However, Fizeau had at least moved the measurement from space to Earth. What was needed, now, was a still better method.

3
In the Laboratory

IN HIS WORK, Fizeau had had the assistance of another French scientist, Jean Bernard Léon Foucault (foo-KOH, 1819-1868).

Foucault went on to try an experiment, rather like Fizeau's. Instead of a toothed wheel, however, Foucault used a second mirror. Light travelled to the first mirror, was reflected to the second mirror, which, in turn, reflected the light to a certain spot on a screen.

Suppose the second mirror is set to spinning rapidly. By the time the light reaches the first mirror and is reflected back to the second mirror, the second has moved slightly and reflects the light to a different spot on the screen.

From the distance by which the reflected light is displaced by a mirror spinning at a known rate, the speed of light can be determined.

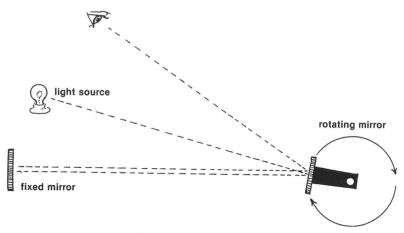

light source

rotating mirror

fixed mirror

Foucault's method

Foucault made his measurements over and over, making various improvements in his equipment. In 1862, he got a result of 185,000 miles per second for the speed of light. This was by far the best figure yet obtained, for it was only a little over 1,000 miles a second below the true value.

Foucault's method had another advantage. It was so delicate that it didn't have to use great distances. It was no longer necessary to use hilltops that were miles apart as Galileo and Fizeau had had to do. Instead, Foucault obtained good results even by using light beams that travelled only about 66 feet together.

This meant he could work in the laboratory, rather than outdoors. What's more; it also meant that Foucault could measure the speed of light when it passed through substances other than air.

As long as light beams had to be ten miles long for the speed of light to be measured, they could only be made to travel through air. Even if you made use of a trough of water five miles long and had a light beam travel from one end to the other and back, you could not determine the speed of light in water. All the light would be absorbed, you see, because water is only transparent over short distances.

Foucault, working with short distances, could measure the speed of light through water.

In his day, there were still two theories about the nature of light. Some thought it to be composed of a stream of particles; others thought it consisted of a series of waves. The wave theory was winning out, but those who accepted the particle theory were not yet completely convinced.

According to the particle theory, light should travel faster in water than in air. According to the wave theory, light should travel more slowly in water than in air.

In 1853, Foucault sent a beam of light through water and measured its speed by his spinning-mirror method. It turned out that the speed of light through water was just about three-quarters that of the speed of light through air. This gave strong support to the wave theory, so that the particle theory was abandoned. (Eventually, half a century later, it became plain that light acted as *both* a wave and a particle, as we shall see.)

When light travels from air into some other transparent material, its pathway is bent, or "refracted," as it makes the crossover. The amount by which it is bent depends on the "index of refraction" of the transparent material. The higher the index of refraction, the slower the speed of light through that material.

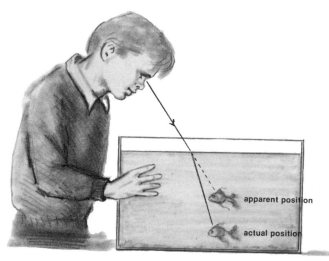

apparent position

actual position

Refraction of light by water

Light travels through water at a speed of about 140,000 miles per second. Through glass, which has a higher index of refraction, it travels at about 125,000 miles per second. Through diamond, which has a very high index of refraction, it travels at a speed of only about 77,000 miles per second.

The next important figure in the determination of the speed of light was a German-American scientist named Albert Abraham Michelson (MY-kul-sun, 1852-1931).

He began working on the problem in 1878, and he made use of Foucault's scheme, but he improved the delicacy of his equipment. Foucault had managed to get the spot of light to be displaced by only $\frac{1}{40}$ of an inch when he used his spinning mirror. Measuring that $\frac{1}{40}$ of an inch accurately was rather difficult.

Michelson got a displacement of 5 inches, which was much easier to work with. In 1879, he reported the speed of light to be 186,355 miles per second. This was a considerable improvement on all earlier figures, for it was only about 73 miles per second too high. For his work on light then and later, he got a Nobel Prize in 1907. He was the first American to get such a prize in the sciences.

Michelson, in his search for better and better values for the speed of light, eventually decided to go back to the hilltop method of Galileo and Fizeau. He didn't have to. The results he got in his laboratory were the best ever. Still, he thought that if he could use the same delicate measurements over a long, long distance, he would get still better results.

In 1923, Michelson picked two mountaintops in California. They were not 5 miles apart as Fizeau's had been, but 22 miles apart. Of course, Michelson was able to produce light beams that were much brighter than those of Galileo, or even of Fizeau. Michelson could use electric lights. That meant Michelson could easily send out a light beam that would still be visible after it travelled 22 miles, was reflected, and travelled 22 miles back.

What's more, Michelson felt he should know the *exact* distance between the two mountaintops, so he could know the *exact* distance covered by the light beam. Saying "22 miles" wasn't good enough. He carefully measured the distance between the spots on which he was setting up his equipment on those mountain tops till he got the distance exact to the nearest *inch*.

Finally, Michelson used a special eight-sided spinning mirror that could produce much more displacement than ordinary mirrors could.

He ran his experiments over and over and, by 1927, he was satisfied that the best figure he could get for the speed of light was 186,295 miles per second. This was indeed a further improvement, for it was only 13 miles per second too high.

Even so, Michelson was not satisfied. Sending a light beam through air introduced a slight slowing effect since air had a tiny index of refraction. The only way it was possible to get the true maximum speed of light was to send it through a vacuum.

Roemer and Bradley had dealt with light travelling through long distances of outer space, and therefore through a vacuum. Their systems of measurement, however, had shortcomings that wiped out any possible advantage of using that vacuum.

Fizeau, Foucault and Michelson had developed more and more delicate methods, but they had always measured light travelling through air. Now Michelson determined to use those delicate measurements to deal with light travelling through a vacuum.

Michelson therefore used a long tube, the length of which he knew to a small fraction of an inch. He pulled just about all the air out of it, leaving a vacuum behind. Within it, he set up a system of mirrors that sent a beam of light back and forth till he had made it pass through ten miles of vacuum.

He made his measurements over and over, keeping it up till he died. It wasn't until 1933, two years after he died, that all the calculations were completed by those who had worked with him, and his final figure was announced.

It was 186,271 miles per second. It was a little

Albert A. Michelson (1852-1931)

more accurate than any other he had announced, but not by very much. It was only 11½ miles per second too low.

Michelson was able to do one more thing with his studies of light travelling through a vacuum.

In objects that have an index of refraction, from the tiny one of air, to the large one of diamond, light with short waves (such as violet light) is refracted more than light with long waves (such as red light). This means that short-wave light should travel a bit more slowly through such substances than long-wave light does.

In a vacuum, however, which has no index of refraction, light of all wavelengths should travel at the same maximum speed. Michelson was able to demonstrate this, so the matter could be taken as actual fact and not just as a supposition.

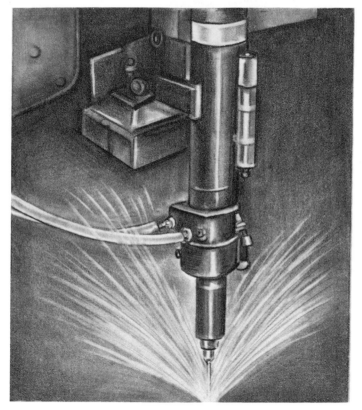

A laser

Even better determinations of the speed of light have been made since Michelson's time. (If not, how would we know that Michelson's best figure is still about 11½ miles per second too low?)

Ordinary light, whether produced by the Sun, by a bonfire, or by a flashlight, contains all kinds of waves of different lengths heading in different directions. In 1960, however, an American scientist, Theodore Harold Maiman (1927-   ) invented the "laser." This produces a light with all the waves of exactly the same length, and all travelling in one particular direction.

With all the light waves of a laser beam possessing the same length, it became possible to measure that length very accurately, as well as the exact number of waves produced in one second. If the length of one wave is multiplied by the number of waves produced in one second, you get the distance light travels in one second.

In 1972, the American scientist, Kenneth M. Evenson, using this method found the speed of light to be 186,282.3959 miles per second. In one second, in other words, light travels 186,282 miles and 697 yards, give or take a yard.

Scientists don't use miles and yards to measure distance. They use "kilometers" instead, where a kilometer is equal to just about $\frac{5}{8}$ of a mile. The speed of light is 299,792.4562 kilometers per second. This is a convenient figure, for it is very close to 300,000 kilometers per second and that is frequently used in rough calculations.

4
Light-Years and the Universe

Now THAT WE have the exact figure for the speed of light, we can point out some facts about the Universe.

The average distance of the Moon from the Earth is 238,867 miles. How long does it take light to travel from the Moon to the Earth? The answer comes out to be just about $1\frac{1}{4}$ seconds.

If, for any reason, the Moon were suddenly to disappear from the sky, the last bit of light it reflected from the Sun would take that much time to travel through space to our eyes, and we would not see the Moon disappear until $1\frac{1}{4}$ seconds after it really did.

The Sun is about 93,000,000 miles from the Earth. It takes light 8 minutes and 19 seconds to travel from the Sun to the Earth. If the Sun were suddenly to disappear, we wouldn't know about it for 8⅓ minutes. It would take light 16 minutes and 38 seconds to cross from one side of Earth's orbit to the other, something Roemer found out when he was timing the eclipses of Jupiter's satellites at different times of the year.

Sun

distance 93,000,000 miles

light takes 8 minutes and 19 seconds to reach the Earth from the Sun

Earth
Moon distance: 238,867 miles

takes light 1¼ seconds from the Moon to the Earth

Distance of Earth from the
Sun and the Moon

The most distant of all the planets is little Pluto, which is nearly 40 times as far from the Sun (on the average) as Earth is. That means it would take light

40 times as long to cross Pluto's orbit as it does to cross Earth's orbit. It would take light just about 11 hours to cross Pluto's orbit.

What about the stars?

The stars are so much farther away from us than any of the planets that it is convenient to use a distance called a "light-year" to describe how far away they are.

A light-year is the distance travelled by light in one year. To see how long such a distance is, let's first see how many seconds there are in a year.

There are 60 seconds in a minute, and 60 minutes in an hour. That means there are 60 × 60, or 3,600 seconds in one hour. There are 24 hours in a day. That means there are 3,600 × 24, or 86,400 seconds in one day. There are 365.2422 days in a year that means there are 86,400 × 365.2422, or 31,556,926 seconds in one year.

In 1 second, light will travel 186,282.3959 miles. In 1 year, then, light will travel 186,282.3959 × 31,556,926, or 5,878,499,776,000 miles. Since the figure 1,000,000,000,000 is "one trillion," a light-year is just a little bit under 6 trillion miles.

It turns out, then, that 1 light-year is equal to nearly 25 million times the distance from the Earth to the Moon. It takes our astronauts 3 days to go from the Earth to the Moon. If they could continue at that average speed it would take them about 200,000 years to go a distance of a light-year.

To put it another way, a light-year is 1,600 times as long as the distance across the orbit of Pluto.

Now we are ready to consider the distances of the stars.

Star map

The nearest star to us is a dim little object called "Proxima Centauri" (PROK-sih-muh-sen-TAW-ree). It is 4.27 light-years away; or just about 25 trillion miles away. There is no star closer to us than that.

This means that the light from Proxima Centauri takes 4.27 years (4 years, 99 days) to reach us. Light, which travels so quickly that it can go from the Earth to the Moon in $1\frac{1}{4}$ seconds, takes 4.27 *years* to reach us from Proxima Centauri.

And Proxima Centauri is the *nearest* star.

Sirius (SIR-ee-us), the brightest star in the sky, is 8.64 light-years away, twice as far as Proxima Centauri.

Rigel (RY-jul), one of the bright stars in the constellation of Orion (oh-RY-un), is 815 light-years away, and is therefore 95 times as far away as Sirius is. It takes 815 years for light leaving Rigel to cross the vast space between us and to reach our eyes. The next time you look at Rigel, remember that the light you see left Rigel on its long voyage when Richard the Lionhearted was a little boy.

Yet even Rigel is a star in our own neighborhood.

The Sun and all the stars we see in the sky are part of a large conglomeration of stars—about two or three hundred billion of them—that is shaped like a pinwheel. This conglomeration is called the Milky Way Galaxy (GAL-uk-see).

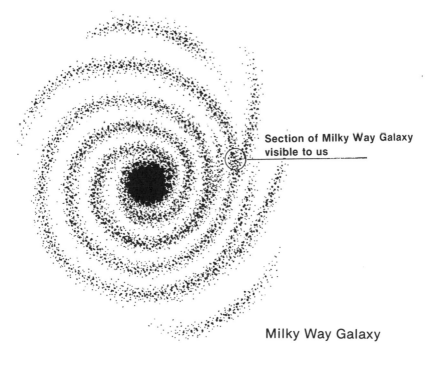

Section of Milky Way Galaxy visible to us

Milky Way Galaxy

We are nowhere near the center of the Galaxy. We and all the stars we see in the sky are about 25,000 light-years from the center. We can't see any light from the center of the Galaxy because there are huge, dark clouds of thin matter between us and the center. However, radio waves from the center can penetrate those clouds and reach us.

The radio waves we can detect from the center right now, left the center 25,000 years ago, long before human beings became civilized.

The entire Galaxy from end to end is at least 100,000 light-years wide, which means that the same light waves that can travel from the Earth to the Moon in 1¼ seconds would take 100,000 years to travel across the full length of the Galaxy.

And our Galaxy isn't all there is in the Universe by any means. There are many billions of other galaxies, most of them smaller than ours and a few considerably larger. The nearest large galaxy to ours is the "Andromeda galaxy" (an-DROM-uh-duh). It can be seen on a clear, dark night as a small hazy patch in the constellation of Andromeda, and it is the most distant object that can be seen by the unaided eye.

It is 2,300,000 light years away from us, and it takes 2,300,000 years, therefore, for light from the Andromeda galaxy to reach us. If you should happen to look at the Andromeda galaxy, the light you will be seeing will have left it long before modern human beings existed. When that light left the Andromeda galaxy, the most advanced form of life on Earth were small human-like creatures in southern Africa, standing four feet high on two legs, but with brains no larger than those of moden chimpanzees.

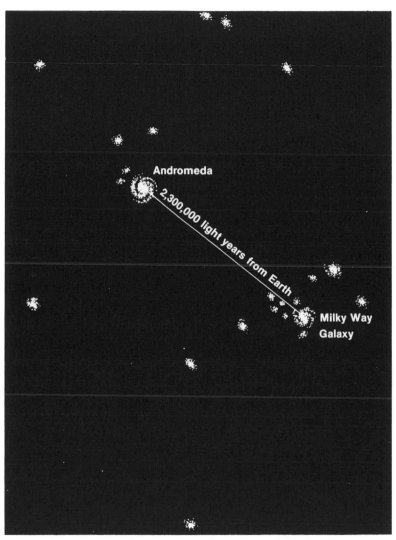

Map of local galaxies

Andromeda

There are many galaxies far beyond the Andromeda. In large telescopes, we can see dim galaxies that are hundreds of millions of light-years away.

In 1963, scientists discovered certain star-like bodies that they called "quasars" (KWAY-zahrz). These quasars turned out to be *galaxies* with very bright centers, galaxies that are so far away that all we can see are those bright centers.

The quasars are the most distant objects known. Even the nearest quasar is about 1,000,000,000 (one billion) light-years away. When we stare at that quasar, we are looking at light that started on its journey when the only living things on Earth were microscopic, one-celled creatures. The light had covered three-fifths of its journey before more complicated life-forms had developed on Earth and were beginning to make their way out onto land. When the light was nine-tenths of the way here, dinosaurs dominated the Earth, and it was 96 percent of the way here before the first human-like creatures evolved.

That is only the nearest quasar. The farthest quasars are over 10 billion light-years away. The light

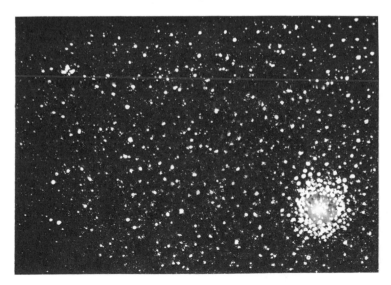

Quasars

from such extremely distant quasars began its journey before our Sun and Earth even existed. In fact, the light had covered more than half the long distance between us before the solar system began to form.

So you see how large the Universe is. Light may travel unbelievably fast when we are dealing with distances on Earth, but when we switch to the Universe as a whole, we find that in comparison with it, light travels at a very, very slow crawl.

Imagine taking billions of years to get from one place to another!

5
Relativity and the Speed Limit

WHEN SCIENTISTS FIRST tried to determine the speed of light, they were merely curious. There was no reason to suppose that the speed of light was anything more than a figure to be determined — like the speed of sound, or of a racehorse.

Just the same, it ended as much more than that. Here's how it happened.

Once it was decided that light consisted of waves, it seemed natural to ask, "Waves of *what?*"

On the ocean surface, there were waves of water. Sound consisted of waves of air. Light, however, passed easily through a vacuum. There was nothing in a vacuum, so what formed the waves of light?

Some people suggested that the whole Universe consisted of an indetectable substance called "ether" (an old Greek word for the material they thought made up the heavenly bodies). Light, they thought, consisted of waves of ether.

That seemed to raise another point of interest. Things on Earth move compared to the surface of the Earth, but the surface of the Earth is also moving. It turns about an axis, but the axis is also moving. The axis moves around the Sun, but the Sun is also moving. The Sun moves around the center of the Galaxy, but the Galaxy is also moving.

Apparently, *everything* is moving, and that seems rather confusing.

It occurred to some people that the ether must form the basic structure of the Universe so it couldn't be moving. It was at "absolute rest." All motions could be measured against the ether and then we would have "absolute motion."

It seemed to Michelson, when he was beginning to be interested in the speed of light that there was a way of measuring the motion of the Earth compared to the ether.

The Earth in all its motions must be moving relative to the ether. Suppose you sent out a beam of light in a certain direction and measured its speed. Since it consisted of waves of ether it would be moving through a motionless substance. If Earth were moving in the same direction, the beam of light would be moving at its own speed plus the Earth's speed, or a bit faster than usual. If Earth were moving in the opposite direction, the beam of light would be moving at its own speed minus the Earth's speed, or a bit slower than usual.

From the difference in speed you could calculate the speed of the Earth's motion against the ether. Once you had the Earth's absolute motion, you could calculate all other absolute motions, by determining speed relative to the Earth.

Of course, the Earth's speed is so much smaller than the speed of light, that adding or subtracting the Earth's speed would make very little difference to the speed of light. How could Earth's contribution be measured?

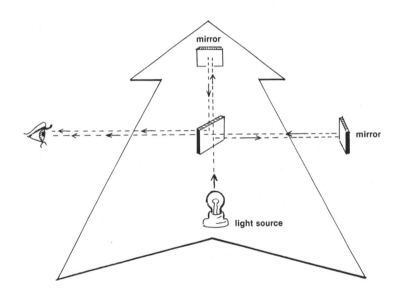

Michelson's experiment

In 1881, Michelson constructed an "interferometer" (IN-ter-fer-OM-uh-ter), that split a beam of light in two, sent the two halves away in different directions, then brought them back together again.

The light in one direction would go with the Earth's motion, then back against it. The light in the other direction would go at right angles to Earth's motion in both ways.

Michelson calculated that if the ether were motionless and the Earth was moving, the two halves of the light beam would travel at slightly different speeds and when they came back together, their waves wouldn't match each other any more.

In some places the waves would reinforce each other, going up and down together, so that the light would be brighter. In other places, the waves would cancel each other, one would go up while the other would go down, and the light would be dim.

In fact, there would be light and dark alternations, or "interference fringes." From the width of the fringes, the difference in light-speed could be calculated and the absolute motion of the Earth could be obtained.

In 1887, Michelson had worked out all the details of what he planned to do, and, with the help of another scientist, Edward Williams Morley (1838-1923), the "Michelson-Morley experiment" was carried through.

As it happened, though, the experiment seemed to fail. There were *no* interference fringes. Light seemed to travel at equal speed in any direction and this didn't seem possible. Michelson ran the experiment many times and always got the same result—no fringes.

In fact, the Michelson-Morley experiment has been run over and over again in the last hundred years, sometimes with equipment much more sensitive than the original. It always ends in the same way. There is no sign of any difference in the speed of light, regardless of the direction in which it moves, and regardless of the way in which Earth moves.

Then, in 1905, a young German-Swiss scientist, Albert Einstein (1879-1955) presented his "Special Theory of Relativity." This offered a new way of looking at motion. Einstein felt there was no such thing as absolute rest or absolute motion. He showed that everything worked smoothly if you always measured motion as compared to something else that was also in motion.

Einstein was not trying to solve the problem of the Michelson-Morley experiment, for it is possible he had not even heard of it. For other reasons, though, it seemed to him that light must always travel through a vacuum at the same speed, no matter in which direction it was going, and no matter how fast or in which direction the source of the light was moving.

For everything else but light, it *does* matter how fast and in what direction the place from which the motion starts is moving. Light, in other words, doesn't act in a "commonsense" way, and most people thought at first that Einstein couldn't possibly be right.

Einstein showed, however, that if light acts the way he thought it should, then all sorts of deductions could be made about how the world ought to behave and how experiments ought to work out. He worked out those deductions and it turned out that those deductions were correct.

Since 1905, scientists have made thousands upon thousands of careful observations of how things behave and work, and they've conducted thousands upon thousands of experiments. Every single one of those observations and experiments backs up Einstein's theory.

Nowadays, all scientists accept the theory as an accurate description of the Universe.

Einstein's theory also showed that light worked in accordance with "quantum theory"—as first worked out by the German scientist, Max K. E. L. Planck (1858-1947) in 1900. Using quantum theory, Einstein showed that light crossed a vacuum because it had particle properties as well as wave properties, and that the ether was unnecessary. Scientists therefore decided the ether didn't exist, and without an ether, it's no wonder that the Michelson-Morley experiment failed.

For their work on the quantum theory, Planck received a Nobel Prize in 1918, and Einstein received one in 1921.

Einstein's theory also made it necessary to conclude that nothing made of matter could go faster than light under any conditions. Nor could any messages ever go faster than the speed of light.

The speed of light, which had till then been looked at as just an interesting figure no different from any other speed, suddenly became a universal speed limit that no one could break.

Till then, human beings had been able to reach out farther and farther by simply learning how to increase speed. At first human beings could go no faster than they could walk or swim. Then they tamed the

Albert Einstein (1879-1955)

horse, and after that they invented steamships and automobiles and airplanes and rockets.

Human beings learned how to cross oceans and continents, first in weeks, then in days, and then in hours. They learned how to speed to the Moon in three days.

If human beings continue to learn how to go faster and faster, can they someday get to the nearest star in three days?

Astronaut on the Moon

No! Human beings can't get to the nearest star in less than 4.27 years, or make a round trip in less than 8.54 years, *no matter what.*

We can't get to the star, Rigel, in less than 815 years or make a round trip in less than 1,630 years, *no matter what!* And if your descendants finally reach Rigel and send a message to Earth that they have arrived, that message will take 815 years to get to Earth, and it will take another 815 years to get a reply, *no matter what.*

We can't get to the center of the Galaxy in less than 25,000 years, or to the Andromeda galaxy in less than 2,300,000 years, or to the nearest quasar in less than 1,000,000,000 years.

Of course, Einstein's theory shows that time slows down with speed. At nearly the speed of light, time slows down to near nothing. You might somehow flash to the nearest quasar and back along with a beam of light and it will seem to you that almost no time has passed.

You will come back, however, to find that 2,000,000,000 years have passed on Earth.

We can no longer dream of exploring the Universe in the usual way. If we leave for the stars, we will probably have to say good-bye forever, and if, for any reason, we can't speed at more than a tenth the speed of light, it is unlikely we will live long enough to reach any destination.

The scientists, from Galileo to Michelson, who tried to measure the speed of light, little knew they were measuring the prison bars that may keep us in the solar system forever.

Index